PRIMARY READERS
STARTERS

Smellybear

John Foley
Illustrator: Elena Selvanova
Cover: Emilio Urberuaga

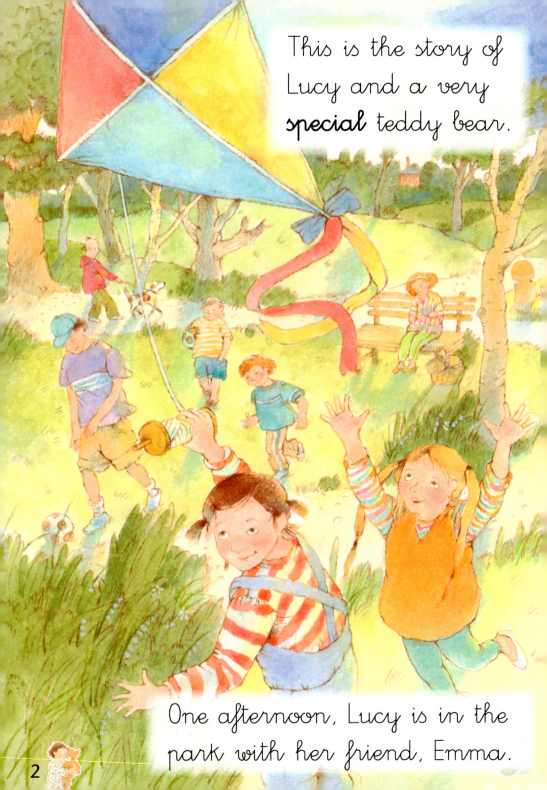

This is the story of Lucy and a very **special** teddy bear.

One afternoon, Lucy is in the park with her friend, Emma.

Now it is raining.
Lucy and Emma
run to the café.

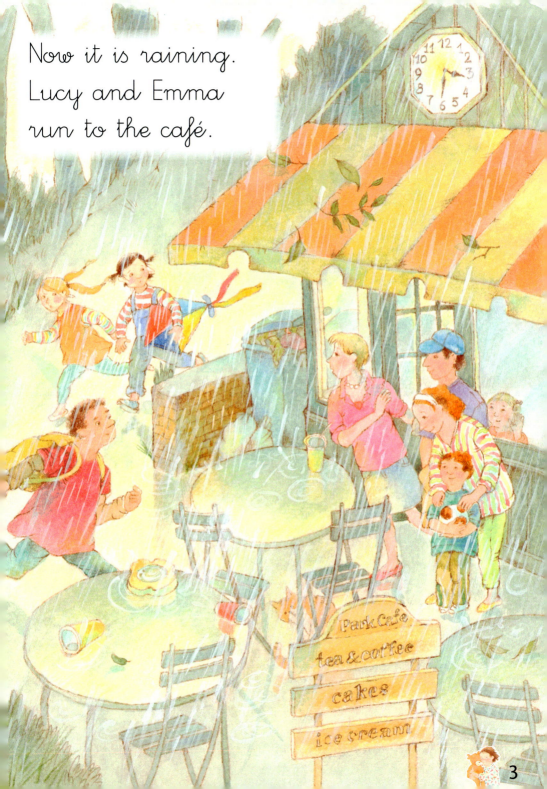

Lucy pulls and pulls and...

Oops! It's a teddy bear! And it's **dirty**.

Now a dog wants the teddy bear too!

But Lucy is the winner!

The bear is **dirty** and **smelly**.

But Lucy likes him. She names him Smellybear...

...and she takes him home.

Now the bear is clean.
And he's **smelly**
in a lovely way!

Mmmm,
I like it here!

13

Now, Lucy's mother is happy.

And Lucy and Smellybear are happy too!

And Smellybear doesn't like the storm.

Lucy and Smellybear run to the door.

Lucy is a very lucky girl...

Picture Dictionary

Picture Dictionary

storm   teddy bear   thunder

want   winner